937
RUT
051411-2

Rutland, Jonathan
See inside a Roman Town.

$10.40

DATE DUE		
JAN 11		
MAR 10		
MAR 11		

SEE INSIDE

A ROMAN TOWN

SERIES EDITOR **R.J. UNSTEAD**

WARWICK PRESS

051411-2

CONTENTS

Series Editor
R. J. Unstead

Author
Jonathan Rutland

Illustrations
Angus McBride
Bernard Robinson
Bill Stallion

Revised edition published 1986 by Warwick Press,
387 Park Avenue South, New York, New York 10016.
First published in 1986 by Kingfisher Books Limited.
Originally published by Hutchinson & Co. Limited 1977.

Copyright © Grisewood & Dempsey Limited 1977, 1986.
Printed in Hong Kong

Library of Congress Catalog Card No. 85-52276
ISBN 0-531-19014-5

Centers of the Empire

According to the legend of Romulus and Remus, the city of Rome was founded in 753 B.C. The city grew in size and power, and by about 140 B.C. Romans ruled all the countries around the Mediterranean Sea. In the middle of the first century B.C. the famous Roman general Julius Caeser conquered Gaul (modern France and Belgium), and invaded Britain. Eventually the Roman Empire stretched from Britain to North Africa, and included most of Europe.

To make it easier to govern their huge empire the Romans built a network of fine roads. They set up fortresses at danger points. And they built Roman towns in all the countries that they ruled. These towns were built partly to provide homes for retired Roman soldiers, and as centers of law and order, and trade. People came to the towns to buy and sell goods, to pay their taxes, and to go to the theater.

But the towns were also designed to show the conquered peoples the advantages of the Roman way of life. As you will see from this book, the Romans were very advanced. Their homes had running water and furnace heating. Their towns were well planned, and inside the strong defensive walls people could feel safe and secure. For several hundred years the Roman towns were islands of civilization throughout the Empire.

On the following pages we shall be looking in detail at a Roman town somewhere in the Empire. We shall visit the baths, the theater, and a temple, look around the shops, watch builders at work, and much more besides.

Above: The ruins of the theater at Pompeii.
Right: A wall painting from a rich Roman villa at Pompeii. The Romans were fond of decorating their houses with scenes from stories about the gods.

A Town Somewhere

A typical Roman town was laid out like a chessboard. The squares were called *insulae* (Latin for islands). Some insulae were filled by important public buildings such as the forum (1 – which combined town hall, law courts, market and meeting place), the theater (5) and the temple (2). The Romans worshiped many gods, so as you can see in the plan there were several temples. In some towns there was also, toward the end of the Roman empire, a church (9). Other *insulae* were made up of houses and shops.

The town was surrounded by thick walls, in which there were four well-defended gates. Outside the walls you can see the amphitheater (8), the aqueduct (12) which carried the town's water supply, the cemetery (10), and, in the distance, a small native settlement (11).

1 Forum	8 Amphitheater
2 Temple	9 Church
3 Baths	10 Cemetery
4 Barracks	11 Native Settlement
5 Theater	12 Aqueduct
6 Inn	13 Gatehouse
7 Circus	14 Villa

The Forum

The forum was the most important public area, and, as you can see in the plan on pages 4–5 it was in the middle of the town. The actual forum was an open courtyard where the townspeople gathered to discuss their town's affairs, or to listen to speeches by the Roman Governor or his officials (who stood on a raised platform, or rostrum). Here also local merchants and farmers from the surrounding countryside set up their stalls, as the forum was also the marketplace. There was usually a shrine in the forum and a drinking fountain. In the buildings around it were eating houses and public toilets.

The forum was entered through an imposing archway. This was sometimes decorated with carvings showing scenes from the story of the Roman Empire. To the left and right of the arch were rows of shops. On the opposite side of the forum stood the most important building – the basilica.

Here, under one roof, were the law courts and town hall. In the picture the basilica has been partly cut away so that you can see the raised platform at one end where the magistrate gave judgment.

Around the great hall of the basilica were the *curia* (the meeting place of the town council), the *tabularium* (where official documents were kept), the treasury, and offices where businessmen met and worked.

This marble statue shows a magistrate addressing the people.

*Below: The forum —
the center of a Roman
town. Grouped around
this marketplace were
all the important
buildings of the town.*

At the Baths

After a morning's work in office, shop or workshop, everyone who could liked to spend the afternoon at the *thermae* (the public baths). Men and women went not just to get clean but also to chat with friends, to exercise in the gymnasium, to play games, and generally to enjoy themselves. Some of the larger thermae even had a library where people could read the Roman equivalent of books – scrolls.

On arriving at the baths the bather undressed in dressing rooms and went first to the *unctuarium*. There he had oil rubbed into his skin. Then, after a spell of vigorous exercise he moved onto the *tepidarium* or warm room, where he lazed around in the warm water pool, chatting to his friends. The bather then moved to the room you can see in the picture – the *caldarium*. Here, in a hot and steamy atmosphere like that of a Turkish bath, he sat and perspired. Attendants served drinks and snacks, and bathers scraped their skin clean with a curved metal tool called a *strigil*.

Next came a dip in the caldarium's hot pool, followed perhaps by a splash in the basin of cold water at the end of the room (you can see this in the big picture).

Then he passed on to the *frigidarium* for a plunge in the cold water swimming pool. And last of all he was massaged (you can see this in one of the small pictures) and had oils and perfumes rubbed into his skin.

Feeling clean and relaxed he might now stroll in the gardens of the thermae, or watch one of the many activities in progress (look at the small picture on the right). These included gymnastics, ball games, and wrestling. For the wrestlers there were slaves in attendance to rub their bodies with oil and to clean and massage them when they had finished.

HEATING SYSTEM

Water for the caldarium's hot pool was heated in huge tanks over a furnace. An overflow from the hot pool carried the cooling water on to the warm pool in the tepidarium. Hot air from the furnace flowed through a hypocaust (a network of channels under the floor – you can see them in the large picture) and up through pipes in the walls to heat the rooms themselves.

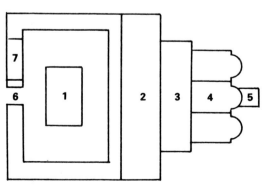

Above right: Wrestlers and athletes in the garden of the baths.

Right: After a cold plunge in the swimming pool the bather was massaged.

Left – plan of the baths: 1 courtyard for games. 2 frigidarium (cold room and bath). 3 tepidarium (warm room and bath). 4 caldarium (hot room and bath). 5 furnace. 6 entrance. 7 toilets.

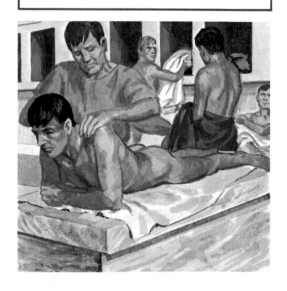

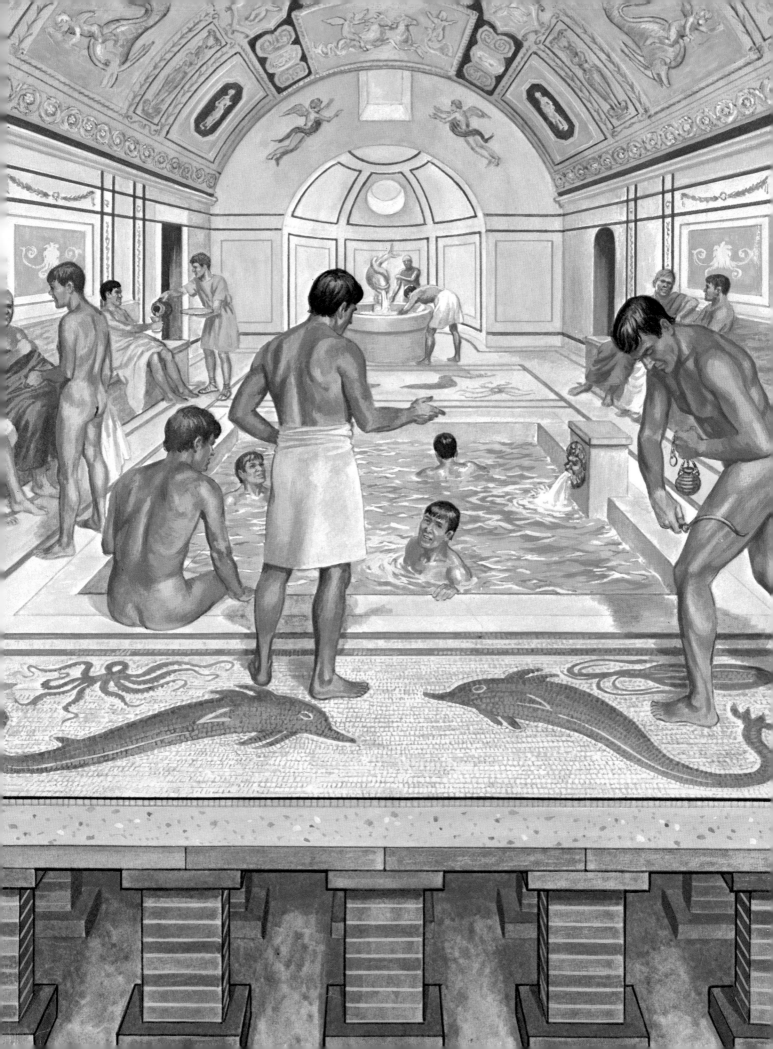

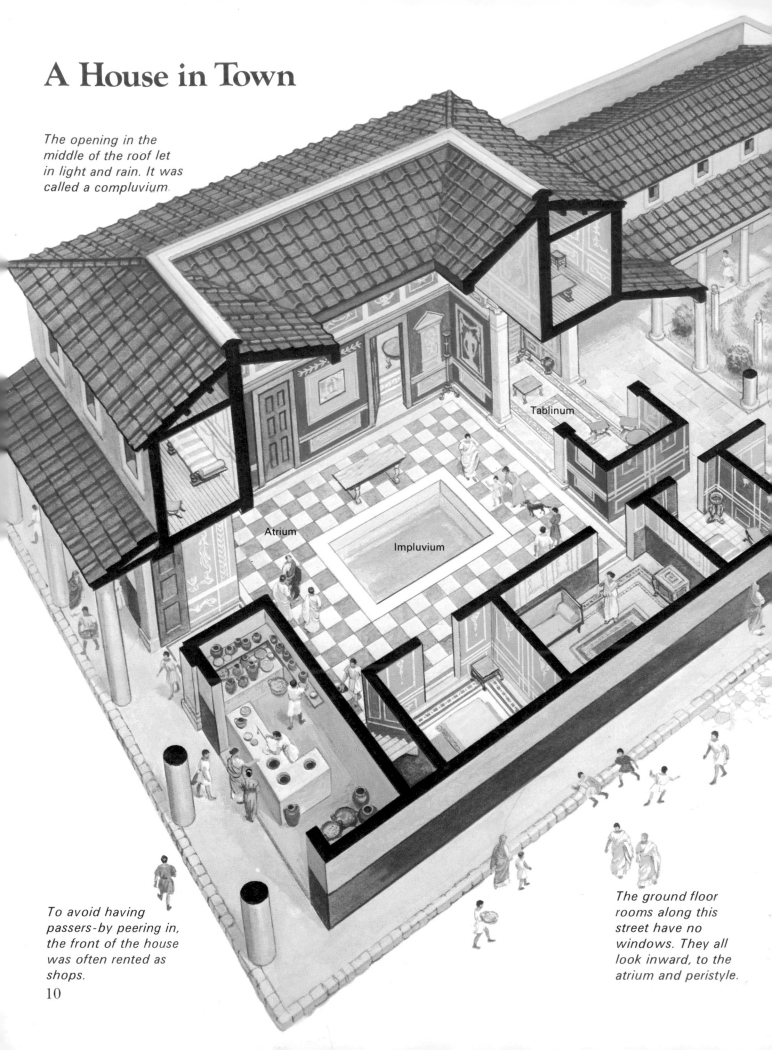

A House in Town

The opening in the middle of the roof let in light and rain. It was called a compluvium.

Tablinum

Atrium

Impluvium

To avoid having passers-by peering in, the front of the house was often rented as shops.

The ground floor rooms along this street have no windows. They all look inward, to the atrium and peristyle.

10

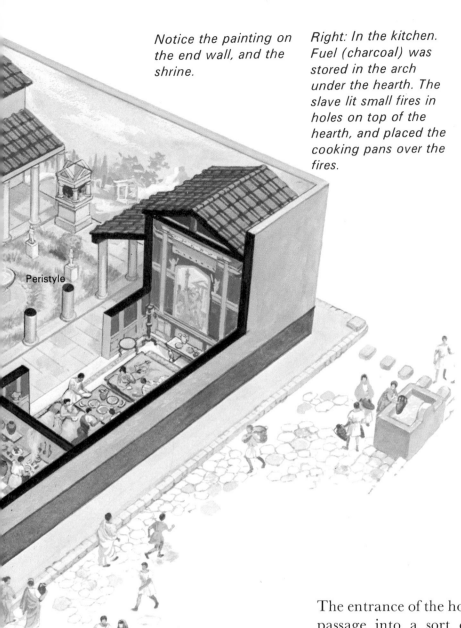

Notice the painting on the end wall, and the shrine.

Peristyle

Right: In the kitchen. Fuel (charcoal) was stored in the arch under the hearth. The slave lit small fires in holes on top of the hearth, and placed the cooking pans over the fires.

You can see the triclinium – dining room – above, on the right side of the peristyle. A slave serves the food and cuts it up. The diners eat with their fingers, lying on couches beside the table. The kitchen is next door, and the toilet was usually next to the kitchen. In this way the water supply and drains were all close together. The drains flowed into the sewer under the street. Although some homes had a piped water supply, most relied on water troughs in the street (you can see one in the picture). The family bathed in the public baths.

ROMAN FOOD

In the early days the main food was a kind of porridge. Later on, people enjoyed lavish feasts which could last several hours. Popular foods included fried chicken, fish, roast meat, and many kinds of vegetable and fruit. No meal was complete without olives, and olive oil was used for frying. In Roman-style cooking the sauce was all important, and might contain pepper, mint and other herbs, celery, dates, honey, vinegar, and wine.

The entrance of the house from the street led through a narrow passage into a sort of inner courtyard – the *atrium*. Here visitors were received, and the children played – except in fine sunny weather. Then the *peristyle* (the open courtyard at the back with its little garden and fountain) was the family's favorite spot.

In the middle of the atrium a pool – the *impluvium* – collected rainwater coming in through the large opening in the roof, called a *compluvium*.

The ground floor rooms on either side of the atrium could be used as storerooms or bedrooms and might include a library. The room at the end (opposite the entrance) was the *tablinium* – a reception room where guests were entertained. Upstairs there were more bedrooms, and the slaves' rooms. These rooms around the atrium often had openings overlooking the atrium as well as ordinary windows.

The homes of the wealthy, like the one in the picture, were heated by a single furnace. The same method was used as at the baths, with hot air flowing through a hypocaust under the floor.

Builders at Work

The peoples of many countries conquered by the Romans built simple homes of wood, straw, mud, and roughly laid stones. The Romans taught them their own more advanced building methods. They had large saws for cutting stone into building blocks, and hammers and chisels for sculpting it into decorative shapes. They had huge cranes for lifting heavy weights. You can see one of these in the background of the picture. For lighter loads they used the simple rope and pulley shown in the picture.

Roman builders molded clay and baked it into bricks and roof tiles. In the picture you can see the two kinds of tile used – flat ones with two ridged edges to form the main surface of the roof, and rounded ones to lay over the ridges and seal the joints. They mixed sand, lime and water to make mortar for joining bricks, or plastering walls – adding stone chippings to the mortar when they needed concrete.

The main walls of a house were sometimes made like a sandwich, with a filling of concrete and outer layers of brick. Another method was to construct a frame of wooden beams, to fill the spaces between the beams with stone and mortar, and then to cover the entire surface with plaster. You can see a workman plastering over a wall like this on the second floor of the house in the foreground.

The columns could be made of solid blocks of stone (as in the background of the picture), but they were often built of bricks and then plastered, as in the foreground.

Some tools used by Roman builders. It is surprising how little the design of tools has changed since Roman times.

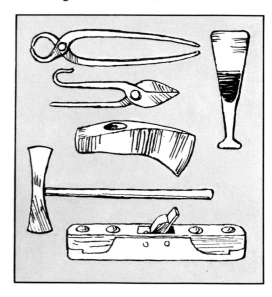

Left: A Roman butcher's shop – from a carved picture, or bas-relief.

Shops and Taverns

Shops, workshops and taverns lined the main streets of the town. On the right of the large picture you can see a tavern selling snacks and hot and cold drinks (these were stored in jugs sunk into the counter).

In the row of shops across the street is a baker, and a butcher. Look at the scales hanging in front of the butcher – a pan hung from one end, and on the other arm of the beam was a sliding weight. The butcher moved the weight out along the arm until it balanced the load in the pan – the distance of the weight along the arm told him the weight. Written on the walls are notices advertising goods. Outside the tavern a wine jar has been painted on the wall.

You can also see steppingstones across the street (useful when the road was wet). The stones were spaced so that cartwheels passed between them. There is also a public water trough. Wealthy men's homes had piped water, but most people got their water here.

Left: A stone flour mill (the flour was made into bread, one of the main foods). Grain was poured in at the top, and was crushed and ground between a fixed stone in the middle, and the outer part – which was turned by two men.

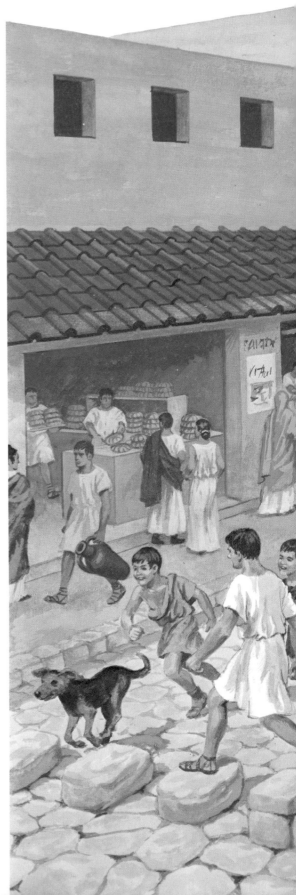

14

A Roman Holiday

On public holidays the people of a Roman town enjoyed a visit to the amphitheater, theater or circus. The spectators at the theater were usually more interested in their favorite actors than in the play. The stars used every trick to win their audience's praise – with elaborate masks and costumes, and with much dancing, music, and mime.

If the play was about someone being killed, then at the last minute the actor's place was taken by a condemned man – who was actually killed on the stage. People of Roman times loved spectacles like this, and flocked to the amphitheater to watch the bloodthirsty "games." There were contests in the arena of the amphitheater between all sorts of wild animals – for example an elephant and a rhinoceros, or a bear and a buffalo. There were contests between an animal and a gladiator (a man trained to fight in the arena).

But most popular of all were contests between men, when two gladiators fought each other to the death. Their weapons included nets, swords, tridents, spears and firebrands – but the two contestants were always armed differently. The excited crowd laid bets on the outcome of each fight. They cheered and booed, and they enjoyed watching the skill of each gladiator much as today people watch that of an athlete.

Left: The Roman theater was shaped like a half circle. The orchestra – the space in front of the stage – was occasionally used by the actors. More often, important members of the audience sat there on comfortable chairs. Both Roman and Greek plays were performed at the theaters.

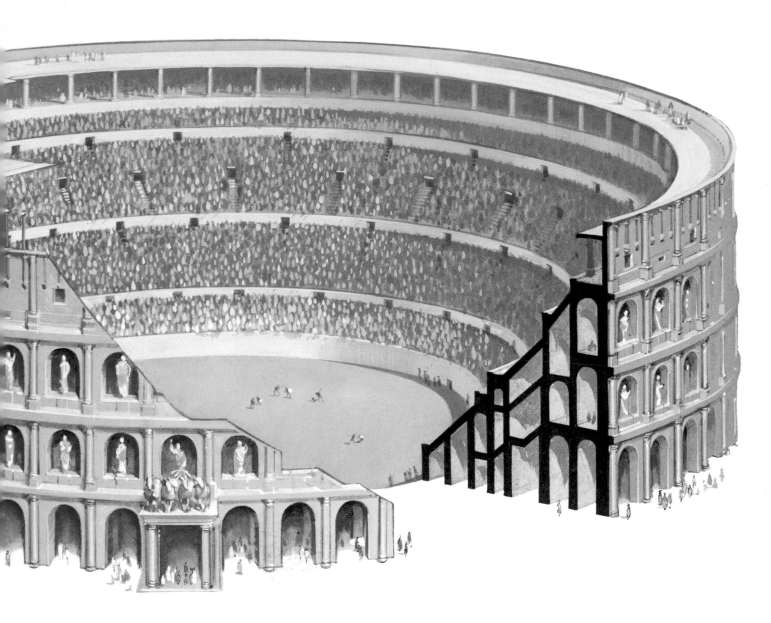

THE CIRCUS

The circus was a huge oval track where chariot races took place. Pulled by two, three, or four horses, the two-wheeled chariots were very light. The charioteer stood up, and one of his main jobs was to balance the chariot – especially when rounding a corner, when he had to lean over like a cyclist.

The races were very exciting and there were often spills and crashes. Many charioteers were killed. Good charioteers were popular heroes.

Above: A big amphitheater like this had seats for 20,000 people or more, but the passages and entrances were so cleverly arranged that the audience could leave quickly. The arena could be flooded for staging mock sea battles. The awning (known as a velarium) above the building shaded the audience from the sun. When it rained, everyone sheltered in the passages.

Centurion Legionary Slinger

ROMAN SOLDIERS

The legatus was a high-ranking officer, in charge of a legion of around 5,000 men. A legion was divided into cohorts and centuries under the command of centurions. Legionaries were all Roman citizens. They were the most important force in a battle, hurling their javelins and then rushing in to attack with their short swords. The cavalrymen and slingers were auxiliary troops, fighting around the edges of the main action.

The only way into the town was through one of the gatehouses. Soldiers could fire down from the towers at attackers outside the walls. Each gatehouse was really a small castle, with quarters for soldiers, and with stores of food and weapons. The main passageway could be blocked by a portcullis. The narrower ones had massive wooden doors. On top of one of the towers you can see a ballista — a powerful weapon which fired large arrows.

The Town's Defenses

The Romans set up forts at strategic points throughout the Empire, from which troops could patrol the countryside. But there was always a danger of a local rebellion, so every town was well protected by a massive wall.

Before the wall was built, a deep ditch was dug, and the earth heaped up to provide a "core" for the wall. The actual stone walls were then built on either side of this core. The inner wall was highest, to make it more difficult for attackers to fire into the town. The wall was around 9 feet (3 meters) thick, and there was a broad wall-walk along which soldiers could patrol and survey the countryside.

The outer wall was often begun well below ground level – to prevent tunneling – and the blocks of stone making up the wall were locked together with metal clamps, so that it was very difficult to break the wall down.

19

Temples and Gods

The Romans worshiped many gods, and each of the temples in the town honored a different one. Most of the temples were quite small, and only the special priests or priestesses and their assistants were allowed inside. People usually gathered outside the temple for worship. There were also temples to the emperor, as it was the duty of a people living under Roman rule to worship him. And there were temples to popular foreign gods such as the Egyptian mother goddess Isis, and the Persian Mithras, lord of light.

20

Religion was very important to the Romans, and every home had a household altar or shrine like the one in the small picture on the opposite page. Here the family worshiped each morning, and on special days they put down offerings of food and wine. The household shrine honored many gods, each of whom looked after different parts of family life.

The Romans believed that their lives were guided by the gods. When they worshiped they hoped to bring themselves good fortune by pleasing the gods. On special occasions they sacrificed animals (killed them at the temple), and removed the liver, lungs, heart, and kidneys. These were examined for signs or omens, and then burned in the altar fire as an offering to the gods.

Above: A sculpted scene of a Roman wedding.
Parents usually chose husbands for their daughters.

Below: The god Neptune. He was at first god of fresh water, but later became god of the sea. His festival was in July, during the hot dry season when rain was needed for the crops.

BIRTH AND MARRIAGE
All sorts of prayers and religious rites were performed when a child was born. A couch and a table of food were prepared for the gods to encourage them to protect the baby. Prayers were said to the many gods who looked after each stage in the child's growth.

Girls often married when they were only 12 years old. The gods were consulted before the day was fixed, and after the wedding there were prayers and a sacrifice.

Left: A cutaway view of a Roman temple. Inside you can see the high priest offering a sacrificed animal to the god. Later the entrails will be examined and burned, and the priest will tell the wor-shipers gathered outside of any omens revealed by the entrails

BORROWED GODS
The Romans borrowed many of their gods and goddesses from the Greeks but gave them new names. The Roman name of Aphrodite, Greek goddess of love, was Venus. Hermes, the messenger of the gods, was Mercury to the Romans, while Zeus became Jupiter.

The Gods and Goddesses of Rome

Throughout their history, the Romans showed a remarkable readiness to welcome and accept foreign cults and religions. Hence, they reverenced a great many gods and goddesses, from those of the early italic tribes and the Greeks to all kinds of dieties worshiped by various peoples whom they conquered.

Religion was central to the Roman home, and every family had a shrine sacred to the household gods, the **Lares** and **Penates,** to whom daily prayers and offerings were made. The Lares guarded the house and the Penates the larder or store-cupboard. Other Gods of the home included **Janus,** god of the doorway, and **Vesta,** goddess of the hearth. In Rome's ancient temple of Vesta, a sacred fire was tended by six maidens, known as the Vestal Virgins.

Most of the important Roman gods were equivalents of Greek deities, such as **Jupiter,** whose temple stood on the Capitoline Hill, and who was equivalent to the Greek god, *Zeus,* king of all the gods; **Juno,** (the Greek *Hera*) his wife, was the sky-goddess. Their family included **Bacchus** (*Dionysus*), god of wine and revels; **Ceres** (*Demeter*), goddess of the harvest, the earth-mother; **Diana** (*Artemis*), the moon goddess and huntress; **Mars** (*Ares*), god of war; **Mercury** (*Hermes*), messenger of the gods and protector of trade; **Minerva** (*Athena*), goddess of wisdom and of crafts; **Neptune** (*Poseidon*), god of the sea, Jupiter's brother; **Saturn** (*Cronus*), god of farming, seed-corn, weights and measures, a gloomy father-figure, whose festival was a time of wild revels; **Venus** (*Aphrodite*), goddess of love and beauty, mother of **Cupid** (*Eros*); **Vulcan** (*Hephaestos*), god of fire, blacksmith and armorer.

In addition to their family gods and goddesses, Romans tended to give a personal nature to Luck and Peace, for example, so their goddesses included **Fortuna,** with her oracular wheel, **Concordia, Flora** and **Roma.** From Julius Caesar's time, emperors were raised to the level of gods and it was a citizen's duty to pay them religious homage. The Christians' refusal to do so brought them persecution under Nero and Domitian.

Among many gods absorbed from other countries were **Apollo,** the Greek god of light, prophecy, music and the arts; **Gybele,** a mother goddess from Asia Minor; **Isis,** the Egyptian goddess of many mysteries and **Mithras,** the Persian god of light, who was especially popular with soldiers. The readiness of the superstitious Romans to accept foreign beliefs assisted the spread of Christianity, which, in spite of official disapproval, was firmly established in every province of the Empire by A.D. 200.

Top right: This famous classical statue of Venus dates from the late 2nd century B.C. It is called the Venus de Milo.

Right: The three Roman gods whose shrines were on the Capitoline, the most sacred hill of Rome. Here they are shown on Trajan's Arch built 114–117 A.D. in Benevento. From left to right: Minerva, Jupiter and Juno.

A Town that was Buried

The scene is the Bay of Naples in southern Italy, near the foot of Mount Vesuvius. The year is A.D. 79. And the writer is an eyewitness, Pliny the Younger. "It was day elsewhere, but there night darker than any night, lightened a little by many torches. ... Flames and the smell of sulfur caused the people to flee." Vesuvius was erupting, and by the end of the second day the town of Pompeii was buried under 20 ft (6 m) of ashes, stones, and cinders. Pliny describes how people running from their homes held pillows over their heads to keep off the "rain" of hot ashes – and how others who took refuge in cellars were choked to death by the fumes. The nearby town of Herculaneum was overwhelmed by a tide of water and ashes which flowed into everything – and then set into a cement-like layer up to 65 ft (20 m) thick.

Much of our knowledge of the buildings and daily life of a Roman town has come from Pompeii and Herculaneum – where life was suddenly halted, and wonderfully preserved under its blanket of ash. When archaeologists began their excavations some 1,700 years later, they found loaves of bread baked shortly before the disaster, and they found hollows in the ashes showing where victims had died. By pouring cement into these hollows they made casts of the bodies, and of other objects.

Today most of Pompeii has been uncovered, and the visitor can see not only the paved roads and big public buildings such as the basilica, temples, and amphitheater, but also private houses, and the homes and workshops of ordinary people.

Overleaf: A vaulted roof in Santa Constanza, Rome, is decorated with a mosaic scene of a grape harvest (A.D. 4).

Above: The remains of the Temple of Apollo, the best preserved temple in Pompeii. It is just one of a number of temples and important buildings which surrounded the large rectangular forum.

Below: An illustration from a guide book to Pompeii of 1881 shows the excavation of a bakery. On the right are millstones which were used for grinding flour and in the background, the oven used for baking bread.

IMPORTANT HAPPENINGS

	Rome and Italy	Europe
B.C. 753	**753** Rome is founded according to the legend of Romulus and Remus. **510** Founding of Roman Republic. Roman nobles drive out their Etruscan kings. **494** Revolt of Plebeians (common people). **493** Roman–Latin Alliance – the Latin League fight the Etruscans. **396–290** Rome conquers other Latin tribes and becomes master of Italy. **264–241** First Punic War. Rome conquers Sicily, a province belonging to Carthage (a city in North Africa). **218–202** The Second Punic War. The Carthaginian general Hannibal crosses the Alps and invades Italy, winning several battles. He fails to capture Rome and returns to Africa in 203. **206** The Romans defeat the armies of Carthage in Spain, which becomes a Roman province in 197. **202** Hannibal defeated at Zama, North Africa. **149–146** Third Punic War. **146** Carthage destroyed. **105–100** Marius consul. **88–82** Civil war between Marius and Sulla. **82–78** Dictatorship of Sulla. **73–71** Slaves' rebellion led by Spartacus. **55–54** Julius Caesar's expeditions to Britain. **48** Civil war between Pompey and Caesar. **44** Caesar murdered. **30** Caesar's adopted son Octavian defeats Mark Antony at Actium, making Egypt a Roman province. **27** Octavian is given the title Augustus and becomes the first ruler of the Roman Empire. **14** Augustus dies. During his time as emperor he brought peace and good government to Rome and to the Empire.	**776** Traditional date of the first Olympic games in Greece. Apollo worshiped at Delphi. **508** Athenian democracy begins. **490** Greeks defeat Persians at Marathon. **460–429** Golden Age of Athens – Greek navy dominates the Aegean. **450** Celtic La Tène culture develops in central and northern Europe. **431–404** Peloponnesian war between Athens and Sparta. Athens surrenders to Spartans. **336** Alexander of Macedon becomes King of Greece; prepares army to defeat Persians. **323** Alexander dies – end of Great Age of Greece. **215–168** Romans involved in wars in Greece. **146** Romans destroy Corinth and make Greece and Macedonia into one province. **87** Sulla defeats King Mithridates of Pontus and takes Athens. **70** Pompey clears the Mediterranean of pirates. **58–49** Julius Caesar's campaigns in Gaul.
A.D. 14	**14–37** Reign of Tiberius. **37–41** Reign of Caligula. **41–54** Reign of Claudius. **54–68** Reign of Nero. Rome destroyed by fire. **98–117** Trajan expands Empire to its greatest extent. **117–138** Hadrian improves frontiers and travels ceaselessly to bring stable government to provinces.	**15** Roman Empire extended to upper Danube. **9** Barbarians defeat Romans at battle of Teutoburger Forest. Augustus abandons policy of Roman conquest east of the Rhine. **43** The Romans invade Britain, which becomes the Empire's most northerly province. **61** Boudicca's (Boadicea) rebellion in eastern Britain is put down. **101–107** Trajan's wars in Dacia (Romania).
A.D. 476	**306–337** Reign of Constantine the Great. **313** Christianity becomes an official religion of the Empire. **364** Empire divided into Eastern (Byzantium) and Western (Rome). **410** Visigoths sack Rome. **455** Vandals ravage Italy. **476** German leader Odoacer deposes last Roman emperor and is proclaimed King of Italy.	**122** Hadrian's wall built across Britain. **222** Goths, Vandals and other barbarian tribes attack the Roman Empire. **270–275** Goths take Dacia. **287** Franks invade Gaul. **370** Huns from Asia invade Europe. **410** Last Roman troops withdraw from Britain. **432** Mission of St. Patrick to Ireland. **449** Jutes under Hengest and Horsa invade Britain. **452** Attila and Huns invade Gaul, Italy. **470** Huns driven out of Europe.

Near East	East Asia	
705 Sennacherib becomes King of Assyria (to 682). Establishes his capital at Nineveh in 701. **670** Assyrians invade Egypt. **612** Medes and allies overthrow Assyrian Empire. **605–562** Nebuchadnezzar II rules as King of Babylon. **539** Cyrus of Persia conquers Babylonia. **525** Persians invade Egypt. **486–465** King Xerxes rules the Persian Empire. **360** Revolts in Persian Empire. **334–330** Alexander the Great defeats the Persians in Asia Minor and Syria, takes Jerusalem, founds Alexandria in Egypt and, with the capture of Babylon, destroys the Persian Empire completely.	**722–256** Eastern Chou Dynasty: Golden Age of Chinese philosophy; "Warring States" period. *c***600** Early cities around river Ganges, India. **563** The Buddha born in Nepal, India. **551** Chinese philosopher Confucius born. **533** Persians invade India, by now highly civilized, with towns, cities and extensive overseas trade. Northwest India becomes a province of Persian Empire for 200 years. Introduction of Persian art and religion. **327** Alexander the Great invades north India. **305** Chandragupta drives Greeks from India; founds Mauryan Empire. **274–232** Emperor Ashoka reigns in India; Buddhism becomes widespread. **221–206** Ch'in Dynasty in China; Great Wall completed. Huang Ti imposes military rule. **206** Western Han Dynasty begins in China (lasts until A.D. 8). Period of great achievement. *c***185–A.D. 320** Invaders (Asiatic Greeks, Scythians, Parthians and Kushans) settle in north India and Punjab. **140–87** Han Emperor Wu Ti conquers Manchuria, Korea, southern China, makes contact with Vietnam, India, and Rome.	**B.C.** **753**
167 Jews under Judas Maccabeus revolt against rule of the Seleucids (a Syrian Dynasty).		
65–63 Pompey conquers Syria and Palestine.	**52** The Huns become subject to the Chinese emperor.	
37 Mark Antony marries Cleopatra, Queen of Egypt.	**AD 2** Chinese population exceeds 60 million. Under firm government, agriculture, mining, literature, science, and astronomy flourish.	
4 Probable date of the birth of Jesus Christ. **27** Baptism of Jesus by John the Baptist. **30** Christ crucified. **45** St. Paul begins his missionary journeys. **66–70** Jewish revolt. Jerusalem destroyed by Titus. Dispersal of the Jews. **116** Trajan extends the Roman Empire to the river Euphrates. **267–273** Zenobia, Queen of Palmyra, rebels against Rome. **286** Division of the Roman Empire; Diocletian and Galerius rule the east. **330** Founding of Constantinople by the emperor Constantine on the site of Byzantium. **447** From Asiatic steppes, Attila and Huns invade the Eastern Empire.	**9–23** Wang Mang usurps the throne of China. **25–220** Eastern Han Dynasty begins in China. **60** Entry of Buddhism into China from India. **78–102** Kaniska, a Kushan King, rules large prosperous kingdom of northern India. **92–192** Period of decline in China as imperial family and national army become more powerful than the emperor. *c***100** Mongols from Korea settle in Japan; Yamato clan wins supremacy. **220** Han emperor of China deposed. **220–580** Period of the Six Dynasties; China divided. **250** Barbarians from north established in southwest Korea. Chinese colonies in Korea extinguished. **320–535** Gupta Dynasty in India; a Golden Age of art, science, literature, and mathematical knowledge. **360–390** Japanese empress Jingo sends troops to invade Korea. **465** White Huns dominate northern India.	**A.D.** **14** **A.D.** **476**

GLOSSARY OF TERMS

Aedile An official in local government.

Amphora A jar for storing liquids such as olive oil.

Aqueduct A channel for carrying the mains water supply to a town; usually carried above ground on arches of brick or stone.

Atrium The entrance hall.

Auxilia Auxiliary troops, recruited from the provinces; they provided nearly all the cavalry and specialist infantry, such as archers and slingers.

Barbarian This word was used by the Romans for all foreigners who were not part of the Roman Empire.

Biga A small chariot pulled by two horses.

Britannia The Roman Province of Britain, invaded by Caesar in 55 B.C., but first conquered by the emperor Claudius in A.D. 43.

Caldarium The hot room at the baths, with the hottest pools.

Cardo One of the two main streets of a town, running north-south.

Castrum A military camp.

Catacomb Underground tunnels and chambers where tombs were placed.

Censor An important government official. One of his jobs was to keep a list of all citizens – this is the origin of our word census.

Centurion An army officer in charge of a century.

ROMAN NUMERALS

Remember that the Romans used Roman Numerals. I = 1, II = 2, III = 3, IV = 4, V = 5, VI = 6, VII = 7, VIII = 8, IX = 9, X = 10, XX = 20, L = 50, C = 100, M = 1000. Today we use "Arabic" numbers, with different columns or places for units, tens, hundreds . . . and with the sign 0 to show an empty column. The Romans had no sign for zero, which made sums much more difficult than they are for us. Try working out XX times XXIV without using our numerals, or even something easy like adding IX and XI.

Century A unit of the Roman army, of 60 to 80 men. A cohort was divided into six centuries.

Clepsydra A water-clock.

Clientes Poor citizens who depended on the favor of a rich man. Each morning, clientes visited their patron, in hopes of receiving a gift of food or money. Rome itself had clientes – independent states who accepted the overlordship and protection of Rome.

Cloaca A large underground drain or sewer.

Cohort A unit of the Roman army of around 400 to 600 men.

A legion was divided into ten cohorts.

Compluvium An opening in the roof of a house to let in light and rain water.

Consul The top government official in the Roman Republic – equivalent to a prime minister. Until the end of the Republic, two consuls were the supreme heads of state. They were elected each year: their duties were to make sure that the laws were obeyed, and to lead the army in time of war. Under emperors the powers of the consuls grew less but the consulship was still

---

ROMAN MONEY

The main coins were the bronze as and the silver denarius. At first the denarius (the word comes from the Latin word for ten) was worth 10 asses, but later it was valued at 16 asses.

There were also the quadrans (¼ as), the semis (½ as), the dupondius (2 asses), the tripondius (3 asses), and the sestertius (a silver coin worth 4 asses). The aureus, a gold coin, was worth 25 denarii.

At first Roman coins had a wide variety of illustrations, but Julius Caesar began the tradition, still followed, of showing the ruler's head on one side.

thought of as a supreme honor.

Curia A meeting place where government affairs were discussed.

Decamanus One of the two main streets of a town, running east-west.

Dictator In the early Republic, a dictator was a general appointed to rule the state during an emergency. This term of office lasted only six months. Much later, men like Sulla and Caesar called themselves dictators – but this was really an excuse to force Romans to obey them.

Frigidarium The cold room at the baths, with the cold water swimming pool.

Gladiator An armed man who fought to the death in the amphitheater – most were criminals, slaves, or prisoners of war.

Gladius A short sword.

Groma An instrument used by surveyors when marking out straight lines for roads and so on.

Hypocaust An under-floor heating chamber. Hot air from a furnace passed under the floor and up the sides of the room through hollow tiles.

Impluvium A pool built into the floor of the atrium to collect rain water falling through the compluvium.

Insula One block or square in the chessboard layout of a Roman town. The word was also used for a block of apartments.

Legatus or legate. The commander of a legion. In the Republic the legatus was the chief assistant of the governor of a province.

Legion The largest division of the Roman army, with 4,000 to 6,000 men. It was divided into ten cohorts. These were supported by cavalry and lightly armed troops. Augustus divided the army into 28 legions. Every legion had its own standard, a silver eagle, which it carried into battle.

Lictor An official working for a magistrate. He carried a bundle of sticks called the fasces as a symbol of Roman authority. His job included summoning offenders, and carrying out their punishment.

ROMAN EMPERORS					
B.C. 23	Augustus	**235**	Maximin Thrax	**293–296**	Constantius Chlorus
A.D. 14	Tiberius				
37	Gaius (Caligula)	**238**	Gordian I, II, III	*293–311*	*Galerius*
				305–307	Flavius Severus
41	Claudius	**244**	Philip and others		
54	Nero			**308–324**	Licinus
68–69	Galba	**249**	Decius and others	*306–337*	*Constantine I*
69	Otho and Vitellius	**253**	Gallienus and others		(Sole Emperor of East and West, **324**)
69	Vespasian			**337–340**	Constantine II
79	Titus	**268**	Claudius II	**337–350**	Constans
81	Domitian	**269**	Aurelian and others	*337–361*	*Constantius II*
96	Nerva			*361–363*	*Julian*
97	Trajan			*363–364*	*Jovian*
117	Hadrian	**275**	Tacitus	*364–375*	*Valentinian I*
138	Antoninus Pius	**276**	Probus	*364–378*	*Valens*
		282	Carus	**367–383**	Gratian
161–180	Marcus Aurelius	**283**	Carinus and Numerian	**375–393**	Valentinian II
				379–395	*Theodosius I*
176–192	Commodus			**385–388**	Maximius
193	Pertinax			**392–394**	Eugenius
193–211	Septimius Severus		Empire split into four sections under two Augusti and two Caesars	**395–423**	Honorius
				425–455	Valentinian III
198–217	Caracalla			*457–474*	*Leo I*
217	Macrinus			**475–476**	Romulus Augustulus
218	Elagabalus				
222	Severus Alexander	*284–305*	*Diocletian*	Eastern emperors in *italics*	
		286–305	Maximian		

Magister A teacher.

Magistrate One of the elected officials who governed Rome during the Republic. The two consuls were the chief magistrates. Below them were two or more praetors, who judged law cases, two quaestors, in charge of finance, and two aediles, who took care of the day-to-day running of the city. Every five years two very important magistrates, the censors, were elected to record the exact number of citizens, and the amount of property each citizen owned. Under the emperors, Roman magistrates lost most of their power.

Orchestra The semicircular space in front of the stage in a Roman theater.

Palla A woman's cloak. It was wrapped around the body like a toga, and one end could be draped over the head.

Patrician A wealthy nobleman.

Peristyle A courtyard or garden surrounded by an arcaded walk.

Pilum A Roman soldier's javelin.

Plebeian The plebeians or "plebs" were the common people, such as farmers, craftsmen and traders.

Praetor A magistrate or judge.

Praetorian Guard The household troops of the Roman emperors. There were nine cohorts – about 5,400 men – stationed in and around Rome. They were commanded by two Prefects, appointed by the emperor.

Prefect During the Republic, a prefect was a man chosen by a magistrate to be his second-in-command. Under the empire, however, prefects were appointed directly by the emperor himself. Prefects governed Rome, the Praetorian Guard, and overseas provinces — all in the emperor's name.

Proconsul A governor or military commander of a Roman province.

Province From the Latin *provincia* (area of command). A province was conquered territory ruled for the Roman people by a magistrate.

Quadriga A large chariot pulled by four horses.

Quaestor An official in charge of money matters.

Senate A council of some 300 important citizens. In law, its taskwas to advise the consuls; in fact, for a long time the Senate practically ruled Rome. Julius Caesar weakened the power of the Senate; under the Empire, it became more and more the puppet of the emperor.

Stilus This was used for writing on wax tablets. One end was sharp, for writing – the other end was flattened, for rubbing out.

Stola The long flowing dress worn by women. It was gathered in at the waist, and fastened at the shoulders with clasps.

Strigil A curved scraper used for cleaning one's skin at the Baths.

Taberna The Latin word for a shop, booth, stall, inn, tavern.

Tepidarium The warm (tepid) room at the baths with the warm water pool.

Thermae The Roman name for the baths.

Toga The flowing garment worn by men, made of a large circular piece of woolen cloth. There were various types of toga: the toga praetexta, for

Many town-dwellers lived in apartments. This is a model of a block.

example, had a broad purple stripe around the hem. Senior magistrates wore it.

Tribunes Representatives of the Roman people. The first tribunes were elected in 490 B.C.

Triclinium Dining room.

Tunic The usual garment worn by men and women. It was held at the waist with a belt, and at the shoulder by clasps. It was rather like a loose dress, was kneelength or longer, and could have sleeves or be sleeveless.

Velarium A canvas sun roof or awning used to shade spectators at the theater and amphitheater.

Via The Latin word for road.

Vigiles Night watchmen whose special duty was to fight fires.

ROMAN MEASURES

Measures of length were based on the body. They included the digit (finger), palm, foot, pace (two steps), and cubit (forearm). Four digits equaled one palm, four palms equaled one foot, five feet equaled one pace, and 1000 paces equaled a mile. The Roman foot was 11⅝ in (296 mm), and the Roman mile was 1618 yards (1480 m).

Weight was measured in unciae (ounces) and librae (pounds). The Roman pound equaled 11½ oz (327·45 g). The sextarius was the unit of volume, and was just under 1 pint (0·53 liter). For larger volumes the unit was the amphora (48 sextarii).

For measuring areas of land, the iugerum (120 ft by 240 ft) was the standard unit.

INDEX

PHOTOGRAPHIC ACKNOWLEDGEMENTS
The publishers wish to thank the following for supplying photographs for this book: Page 2 Italian State Tourist Office; 3 Ronald Sheridan; 6 Mansell; 14 Mansell; 19 Mansell; 21 Mansell *top*, Sonia Halliday *bottom*; 22 Musées Nationaux, Paris *top*; Mansell *bottom*; 23 Sonia Halliday; 24–25 Michael Holford; 28 Mansell; 30 Mansell.

Picture research: Jackie Cookson